READ

NOTHING

IN HERE

21 THINGS YOU SHOULD KNOW
ABOUT NOTHING

"THE MINUTE YOU START WONDERING WHAT NOTHING IS AND CAN BE, YOUR THINKING OPENS UP."

1

YOU CAN'T WRITE A BOOK ABOUT NOTHING

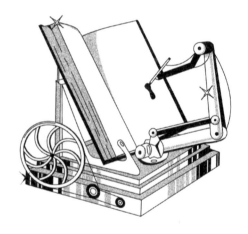

For you the word nothing might sound like a fart in the wind. A useless word that no one would bother to think about. You might have forgotten that the greatest mathematicians in the world have struggled with the question of where nothing begins and where it ends. The most brilliant philosophers have examined the meaning of nothingness for ages. Some of the world's greatest thinkers have been racking their brains on whether or not there even is such a thing as nothing. And me? I've spent two whole seconds investigating this matter and read one page on the Internet. Yes, I think it's fair to say that I'm an expert on nothing.

This book is my attempt to save the world. Before we all turn into t-rexes, stuck to our computers and thinking we know everything. Must you feel immortal now that Google is your best friend? You probably think it's more important to have access to information than to really know stuff. And that it's not important to own information, as long as it's within reach – right? I agree. But when it comes to this subject, Google isn't going to help you. It's the one thing that Google simply doesn't have an answer to. What you and I think of nothing might be more important than what search engines can ever tell you. This just might be that one thing you haven't thought about. Its true meaning may have never crossed your mind. I'm on a mission to make you know everything about nothing.

Why would you want to know everything about nothing? After all, nothing might just simply be what it is: nothing. Let me explain. We all have different interests. One person might be an expert on art because he's read everything about it, perhaps even created some art himself. Someone else might be an expert on virtual reality because he's been following these innovations for ten years. Nowadays, whatever interests you makes you an expert. Being an expert basically comes down to how much time you've been occupied with something. Which underlines my point: being an expert isn't even a cool thing anymore. Saying you're an expert is basically saying that you have enough information. That you know everything. That's why this crazy weird thing called nothing is so important. It is connected to virtually everyone's interests. It has to do with art, it has to do with mathematics, marketing, innovation, psychology, language, creative thinking and more. That's why I like to say that it's also of interest to everyone. If you can't connect to nothing in the different ways it reaches out to you, it must be a deliberate choice. Nothing is literally connected to you in a thousand ways.

In addition, as a copywriter and a creative, for me the most exciting thing in the world is to write a book about nothing. All other books are about something. Some books discuss nothing in a spiritual way. Or in a way that no one understands – meant for scientists or other brainiacs. No one really talks about nothing the way I'm going to in this book. Which is basically like a 5-year-old, because I'm going to be posing many questions about nothing. That's what makes this the first real book about nothing. Just imagine if I succeeded in doing that! How crazy would that be? "No, no – it's absolutely impossible to write a book about nothing." That's what everyone told me. Which has only encouraged me more to fill these pages.

When you're writing a book about nothing, you notice
that the word nothing is everywhere. You also notice that
brands use and misuse the word quite often. Once I was
staring at a funny bottle of juice that claimed to be full
of nothing. I thought this had to have been a joke by the
manufacturer, and imagined how funny it would be to test
whether imaginary juice would sell as well as real juice.
However, they meant something completely different by
"full of nothing", namely 'no added sugar'. Which doesn't
mean there isn't any sugar in it, they just didn't add any
more of it. You see how confusing the word nothing is?
It's horrible, questionable, but above all, it's wonderful.
Perhaps the confusion intrigues me. I'm not even sure
whether I believe in nothing.

It's great to see that more people value nothing
nowadays. I mean, you can't write a book about nothing
without valuing nothing. Giving new meaning to it. It's
quite challenging, to say the least. The book sort of
wrote itself the minute I started valuing nothing. Simply
put, I had never not considered nothing to be nothing.
The minute you start wondering what nothing is and

could be, your thinking opens up. I started writing about nothing after staring at a blank page for hours and hours. Something I had never done before. It was quite inspiring. I noticed the texture of the paper. I realized I had never really looked at paper this way before. It has a distinct smell, too, which got me wondering what nothing would smell like? What would it feel like? What does it mean to think nothing? What if we do nothing all day long?

These are questions an imaginative kid could easily answer. But we're not kids and I think we can all agree that this Google generation isn't exactly imaginative. So I'm here to spell it out for you. I will explain how important nothing is. And that nothing is actually quite important. It's a confusing topic, I have to admit. You can read this book by taking everything literally and then it's just, well, a confusing book about nothing. You can just have a good laugh, because of all the different ways in which I make you look at nothing. Or you can try to poke your brain a bit and learn something about nothing. However you decide to read this, it's your decision – I have nothing to do with that.

"SPACE
JUST SEEMS
LIKE A BORING
NOTHINGNESS
TO ME."

2

EVERYTHING STARTS WITH NOTHING

Before breakfast. Before the Internet. Before your mobile phone. Before this book. Before us humans. Before there was life, there was nothing. About 14 billion years ago, the beginning of things started with nothing. Then all of a sudden there was this Big Bang. They call this the birth of the universe, also known as 'all of space and everything in it'. This led to the Earth, where organisms prevailed and mammals emerged. Millions of years later, these evolved into a hyperintelligent species (with a few exceptions, of course). Fantastic story! But let's be honest: were you there to witness any of this? I mean, no one saw the Big Bang or heard it (I imagine there was a loud noise). I have my doubts about this story...

Luckily, there's also another story. Depending on where you live, people tell this one slightly differently. Here goes the quick version. Out of nothing came a man who created Heaven (like iCloud, but then for people) and Earth in six days. He filled his Earth with plants, organisms, and animals. And on the seventh day, he decided to put humans (giant USB sticks with legs) in charge of his world – so they could rule over all creatures. My problem with this story is that no one actually knew the man, nor did anyone have a conversation with him. I believe some people talk to him, but it's not a real conversation like you and I could have. I also have my doubts as to whether this would be a man, since for most men it would just be impossible to multi-task between plants, organisms, and animals. It just seems illogical. Religious or not, nothing must be really inspiring to people. *Ex nihilo nihil fit* – which means 'out of nothing comes nothing' – is a Latin phrase to explain the existence of Earth and life. Although many people (believers and non-believers) interpret this phrase in different ways, it's generally used to argue that a world cannot emerge without there being a creator; a world can't just be created out of nothing. However, I think it's impossible to pinpoint where nothing starts and where it ends. If you say "out of nothing comes nothing" or "nothing was ever born from nothing", you are basically saying that Earth doesn't have a beginning and everything on it has just always been there. But what do you call that moment right before everything? To me 'ex nihilo nihil fit' means the exact opposite; that things can come out of nothing.

Then there's a third story. That we are descendants of aliens! Every plant, tree, insect, and animal is made of meteors and chunks of other planets. And that aliens have put human-like creatures on Earth to investigate our world – to make other planets better and basically to learn from our mistakes. This means we're simply imported from other planets without even knowing it. After years and years, we've grown so accustomed to Earth that we have started believing we're earthlings.

Indian Sanskrit texts and Egyptian drawings describe and

depict flying objects and mysterious creatures; these might not be gods, but aliens! It would be pretty smart, though, making creatures believe you own the planet and then, after a while, start digging all sorts of valuable resources out from under them, such as diamond and gold. Seems similar to how we treat ants. We notice them, we step on them whenever we want, and we study their behavior, their strengths and weaknesses. The only thing the aliens didn't take into account is that we would start destroying Earth the minute we started consuming it. Unlike ants, we're consuming more than we're creating. Don't worry; there are thousands more planets like this one. Some even better preserved. Our world might just be a speck on the map, but what I do know is that aliens must find our planet pretty interesting compared to the boring nothingness of space.

If the above is indeed the case, all those sci-fi movies had it completely wrong. Aliens are not sophisticated creatures from sophisticated planets. They are bored minimalists. Entities that have learned how to live with nothing, and simply came to our planet because we have lots of everything! So far, this story seems the most reliable one to me. I can see that certain people are not from this planet; I might even know a few myself. However, there's one thing I can't get my head around. If we are aliens, then what do we call those creatures with big eyes and big heads, who visit our planet with UFOs? And why would they leave these big crop circles behind on Earth? A sticky note would be so much easier. It just doesn't make any sense to me.

Whatever story you believe (or maybe you have a better one), each of these stories start with nothing. No one seems to pay attention to this. What was there before creation? I will probably give you an unsatisfying answer, but you will have to be a bit more patient before we get there. Answering this question isn't as easy as it might seem. We first have to set out what it is that we currently think about nothing. So far, we don't appear to have thought much about it at all. Some people don't even have an opinion about it. If I would ring at the door of a random person and ask him "Excuse me, sir, what do you think about nothing?" I doubt I'd get a useful answer. "Why would you even think about nothing? Isn't that a waste of time?" Indeed, it's a beautiful waste of time. It's the kind of waste that we can recycle our thinking with.

"IF YOU THINK
YOU KNOW
NOTHING, YOU
MIGHT BE RIGHT."

3

EXPERTS KNOW NOTHING ABOUT NOTHING

If you think you know everything about nothing, you're probably wrong. But if you think you know nothing, you might be right. Nothing is the kind of notion astronauts talk about on a boring day in space, floating around and philosophizing about dark matter. It would certainly be the right place to talk about this, since 74 per cent of space is made up of dark energy and considered to be nothing. I'm not even sure what dark matter exactly is and neither are the scientists. I only know that it matters to a lot of people. In short, nothing is something we haven't really figured out yet. Time and again, the discussion seems to go back to where life started.

The Pirahã might have the answer. They are a fascinating Amazonian tribe and have no words for numbers, days, weeks, months, or years. They're probably the only group on Earth that linguistically lives in the now. The Grammar of Happiness follows the story of author and researcher Daniel Everett spending time among the Pirahã tribe. He discovered that this tribe only has a sense of living history: whatever they remember themselves. There are no stories reaching back before living memory, and no creation myths.

Everett asked the Pirahã what they thought the state of the world was before there were Pirahã: "What was the world like long ago, before there were people? Who made the trees and who made the water?" The Pirahã guy just looked at him and said: "What?" Everett repeated: "Who made the trees and who made the water?" He answered: "Nobody made the trees and nobody made the water; they're just trees and it's just water". I think the Pirahã man gives a fair answer. The Earth just is – and why on Earth would you want to explain that?

Scientists, the supposed experts on this matter, can't agree on this either. In the Existence of Nothing – a debate hosted by Neil deGrasse Tyson (famous for his Cosmos – a Spacetime Odyssey series) – several scientists discuss this subject from different perspectives. It's a really fascinating topic, but half of my brain couldn't comprehend what was said and the other half fell asleep. These scientists all have a different definition of nothing and can't even imagine the headache that gives a noob like me.

What I did learn from this debate is that even though you can have a universe with nothing in it, when the laws of physics still apply throughout that universe, apparently it's not nothing. I'm not sure whether I understand this correctly. I imagine that if I had a black box with nothing in it, some sort of energy would still be present, which would then still be something. Now, let's not get too serious with this; even these scientists are not certain of anything.

So, who can help us find answers? In *Write Nothing In Here* I wrote a tiny bit about Parmenides, a Greek philosopher who didn't actually focus on trying to explain what nothing is. However, he basically said that if something is a concept in the mind, it exists. He claimed that it's impossible to refer to nothing. When you're talking about nothing, you are always referring to something. Parmenides said that if we mention things from the past, they must always be existent now as well, even if it's just as a manifestation of our minds. When something is a thought, it is already existent. This is way less complicated than what some other philosophers came up with, and I like how he explains truth and reality.

Out of all the things said about nothing, I might agree most with the Nobel Prize-winning philosopher Nicolas Murray Butler. He states that "An expert is one who knows more and more about less and less until he knows absolutely everything about nothing." How could I disagree with this? The true expert knows everything about nothing, because he/she is able to step away, reinvent, and learn more about that what makes him/her an expert.

"OUR WORLD NEEDS MORE INSIDE-THE-BOX THINKERS."

4

I'M SURE WE DISAGREE ABOUT NOTHING

We 'regular people' without PhDs in science also have an opinion about nothing – and we should. In its simplest form regarding our language as we use it every day. Scientists can think whatever they want about nothing, but we use it on a daily basis. We ourselves can decide what it is and what it isn't. My advice? Don't let anyone ever tell you what nothing is. Not even me. I just happened to write a book about it, because I create ideas out of nothing on a daily basis. But it might as well have been you. If you're a lawyer, you probably have a completely different way of using this nothing. Or a salesperson, in which case nothing is just what you need to make a sale.

It is funny to notice that I use this 'nothing thinking' more than I realized. Whenever I used to fool my dog by faking having a cookie in my hand, he always seemed focused and interested in what I was hiding. He could stare at this nothing for hours and even when I would throw this nothing out of the window, he would keep on staring through the window to find it. In a split second, I could convince him that this nothing was something. It's hilarious to me and we do something similar when we use the word nothing. We make others believe it is something.

The reason why the word nothing is interesting, is because it is a noun. Therefore, grammatically, it always refers to something. For example, if you say "nothing is in the box" you are actually saying that there is not something in the box – or that everything is not in the box. Even when you say nothing is missing, you are saying that everything is present.

From the above, we can understand that a box is never really empty. Maybe that's why the phrase out-of-the-box thinker bothers me so much. It's obviously invented for people who think there's nothing of value inside the box. And even when it does turn out to be empty, it can be really inspiring. The term out-of-the-box thinker comes from an exercise popular in the sixties and seventies introduced by a management consultant called Mike Vance. It involved an image of nine dots. The challenge was to connect these dots by using the fewest strokes. In order to do this, you need to step outside of your ordinary thinking pattern. They say Vance invented this exercise to help organizations come up with out of the ordinary solutions to solve problems. In those days, it wasn't as common for companies to brainstorm and use lateral thinking. The exercise helped them think out of the box; outside the regular approach to problems.

Now, decades later, I notice that many unoriginal thinkers use this phrase to encourage others to think more creatively or unorthodoxly. Let's take the Rubik's Cube as an example. Back in the day, you would be considered pretty awesome (read: an open thinker) if you managed to solve it. Nowadays, it's just a matter of remembering all the moves and steps one should take. You can look this up on the web. Of course, it can still be challenging to solve a Rubik's Cube in a short time, but other than that there's nothing to it anymore. It does not make you more or less creative. The irony is that out-of-the-box thinking has become so cliché, we need a new approach.

Our world needs more inside-the-box thinkers: people who question things and no-things. For no reason, but without being afraid to reinvent things. Or invent something based on what is not. These thinkers are more open to looking closely at what could be inside the box. Or what might fit in the box now that didn't fit before. I invite our generation to be inside-the-box thinkers and to look closely at what could be in the box and what things we're missing in it. Even when it's empty.

Nothing is one of those words that evokes many opinions. People who consider nothing to simply be nothing must be furious about this book.

These people would expect a book with literally nothing in it. Empty pages. In contrast, it's actually full of words. On top of that, I'm giving you various different reasons to think about nothing. For me it's just hilarious that you could even be mad at nothing. I guess we all have a different opinion about nothing and that's a good thing. Whatever you think of nothing should be whatever you think of it, even though it might confirm the complete opposite of what you've been taught to believe in. Make sure to always think about nothing on its own, instead of connecting it with any prehistoric or pre-existing thinking you or others may have had before. You might think completely differently about nothing than you did years back and that's fine. I used to have a different opinion about nothing. Disagreeing about nothing is fantastic. It means you're thinking about nothing in different ways.

"WHEN YOU CONSCIOUSLY THINK ABOUT NOTHING, YOU'RE STILL THINKING."

I CAN MAKE YOU THINK ABOUT NOTHING

Let's try something. Think about nothing. Close your eyes if that makes it easier – and breathe in and out. Don't worry, I haven't hidden any booby traps in this book that will punch you in the face. Just give yourself two minutes.

And? Did you succeed? Hard, isn't it? I tried to think about nothing once and, before I knew it, I was thinking about what to have for dinner that night. Then I pictured an empty room and realized this was also something. I tried to picture a dark space and then realized this was simply the same place, but with a lack of light, which isn't nothing either!

When you consciously think about nothing, you're still thinking. Thinking about nothing? It's impossible, because things are all things. You simply can't turn off your brain. Let's try this simpler exercise. Try to do nothing. Stop reading and do nothing for a moment.

Did it work? Did you know that staring is also an activity, as is breathing? It's impossible to do nothing!

I could think up a few more of these useless exercises, but I think you get the point; thinking about nothing is impossible. Thinking nothing is a whole different thing, but equally challenging. Often, when you think you're thinking nothing, your mind wanders off, but you´re still thinking something. Sometimes when people say they're thinking nothing, I just think they can't remember what they were thinking about. Would it be possible to think nothing consciously?

Meditation might be the answer. I've been told you can get into a meditative state by focusing on things and unfocusing. But that doesn't really sound like something one can do in a second. I want to consciously zone out for a moment, like flipping a switch. Is it possible to deliberately think nothing, and just switch off your brain without sleeping? Even when you sleep, your brain is still working. There's thinking nothing of something and then there's perceiving nothing. I can see how drugs could help me achieve the latter state. What about thinking nothing of something, i.e. not judging? Would I have to be really stupid to achieve this? Or does it rather take real intelligence to reach a higher state?

It's impossible to think about nothing and to do nothing. Whether we will ever be able to? Maybe. I would like to believe we will be able to in the future. Perhaps we humans haven't sufficiently evolved to be able to think nothing. Yet. We'll get there eventually. Then we´ll be able to easily reset our brains and make 60-hour workweeks. It would be good for the economy. We normally need a 3-week holiday to recharge; now the same result could be achieved by turning off our brain for a minute. Less people would get burnt out. The streets would be safer because people would be zoning out to get rid of their frustration.

People who meditate are on the right track, though, but it isn't a switch that you can flip on and off. I have never seen anyone meditate in a rollercoaster. What I want is a nothing button and I'm hoping some smart girl or guy reading this might be able to invent one. I don't think it would solely be a spiritual solution; it has to be combined with technology. Spiritual innovation is what I´d like to call it. You'll need a bit more patience, because it's going to take years to invent the nothing button.

For now, the quickest way to think about nothing is actually a really simple one. We have to cheat a little bit, but I'm sure you'll appreciate the irony. Although thinking nothing is impossible, I can still make you think about nothing. If you want to think about nothing, first look at the cover of this book and have a look at the word nothing. Now think about what you just saw. There, you're thinking about nothing. You can do this at any time, wherever you are. When you're feeding the sharks or walking the dog. You can even think about this nothing while driving, as it's completely safe. However, be careful in situations that require your attention such as when you're saying yes to a wedding proposal or when you're in the middle of a job interview.

"I THINK WE CAN AGREE THAT THERE IS MORE THAN ONE NOTHING."

6

THERE ARE DIFFERENT KINDS OF NOTHING

The word nothing brings about an interesting confusion. You might never have thought about it this way, but I recognize 4 types of 'talking about nothing'. The first one occurs during small talk. When you talk about nothing much, such as the weather, the birds, and the bees. The second is when you use it in a conversation on the topic of nothing. For instance, talking about nothing the way I'm trying to do in this book. You really dive into the subject of nothing. The third way is when you use the word nothing, but actually refer to something. People do this all the time. Like "Oh, I'm doing nothing" which is pretty much impossible if you're alive. The fourth one is perhaps the most accurate and truthful meaning of the word. When you're quiet. When you shut up! Only then do you actually 'speak' nothing.

Some would argue that nothing has one definition and would not want to go beyond that. Perhaps this is because, nowadays, we hardly question our word choices anymore. We are increasingly less mindful of our language use. While I'm typing, the accuracy of the word 'mindful' comes into question. In any case, language simply falls victim to our (sometimes sad) human development. The word nothing has developed several meanings, and we humans have become a bit, well, ... lazy in picking our words. It's nothing to worry about, but when you start to use these different kinds of nothing more often, you slowly become a 'nothing thinker'. Good for you.

There's quite a difference between the western and eastern definition of nothing. The Sanskrit word *shunyata*, meaning emptiness, is an important concept in Buddhist culture and is considered to be the ultimate state of mind. Some

Buddhists say that when you've reached this state of nothing, you have sublime focus. I bet they didn't picture a smelly guy on the couch refusing to work or learn anything. Speaking of which, in our western society nothing or emptiness is considered to be an insecurity, a void, or the absence of matter. Something negative. In our society, when you have nothing, you're doing something wrong. I'm sure you can see the irony here. This is the kind of stuff that just blows my mind and makes me even more curious. If Buddhists strive for a minimal lifestyle and maximum awareness, would they be happy without Buddhism? And just to balance things out, there are a couple of other things about us westerners that are also pretty weird.

For example, if you Google nothing, you get at least more than one million search results. I think we can agree that there is more than one nothing. This is entirely your fault, by the way. You keep using the word in different ways. Every nothing means something completely different – it all has to do with the different definitions we have given nothing. I picked a few of my favorites below. Some of these examples have popped up on Google and others are just based on stories that people told me, without realizing how much they were exaggerating by using the word nothing.

Basically nothing is often used in situations where people use nothing in order to sound cool. At the same time, they want to emphasize that they turned a negative situation into a positive one. Like going out on a camping trip with *basically nothing* and still having tons of fun. Or when someone told me about moving to China with basically nothing and then raving about how wonderful it is there. It implies that you don't need a lot to have fun. You can be cool with *basically nothing*.

Virtually nothing seems to be used quite often for when things get out of hand. For example, on the radio I heard about a grandpa who was driving on the wrong side of the highway and there was *virtually nothing* that could stop him, because he had forgotten where he was and lost control over the wheel. *Virtually nothing* can be used to indicate impotence; hopeless situations that have sort of been given up on.

Good for nothing is mostly used in situations when you've done something terrible wrong. When someone considers you utterly useless. You were probably already in the danger zone, but now you've truly shown what you're worth. You're not even good enough for a trash bin, a toilet, or a garbage disposal. You're *good for nothing*.

Thanks for nothing. Wow – where to start with this one? It's a phrase that people say when you've messed up big time. This is the kind of phrase that makes the dog sneak out of the room. It's that last stab in the back when someone is about to leave. Usually at this point, there's no turning back. It's my personal favorite.

The word nothing keeps on developing. It's just a matter of time before another nothing gets introduced to the world. I´d like to introduce a few new ones, so here goes. We'll start with *TGIN*, Thank God It's Nothing. For moments and situations in which you were afraid that something bad would happen, but it turns out there´s nothing to worry about. Next, I´d like to propose *Make nothing work.* When you're given a briefing with very little info to work with. You basically just have to make nothing work.

And finally, as always, the ones that are most fun are those you use out of frustration. So here's one for the hotheads: *Mothernothing!* It's inspired by motherfucker, but that doesn't impress anyone nowadays. You can use Mothernothing! when you're so pissed at someone, you wish he wasn't here anymore. To you he's just the mother of nothing. After reading this book, even this would be a compliment.

"TO ME IT'S QUITE SCARY IF NOTHING SCARES YOU."

7

BACK IN THE
DAY, THEY FEARED
NOTHING

Can you imagine what it would be like to fear nothing? In ancient times, they invented something to describe this fear. It's called 'horror vacui', a Latin phrase that claims that an empty spot or space should always be filled with air or plants. So emptiness cannot and will not exist. This phenomenon is illustrated by many cultures and art styles throughout history. You must have seen those paintings and relics where there seems to be a lack of unfilled space.

But it's not just an art thing. I think it also has to do with the insecure nature of people, who can't live with the idea of having unanswered questions. Where do we come from? How is earth existed? Having no answers to these questions or at least a rough idea is like an empty spot in our mind. Perhaps it's because you have to have some idea or understanding about the world, to function in our world. This seems to be still relevant today. We want to know more stuff; the only thing that has changed is that we want to have answers quicker. I guess this is what makes Google so successful.

There was once a Sultan who took this fear to a whole other level. In the book Nothing That Is author Robert Kaplan mentions that Abdul Hamid II — the long-reigning Turkish sultan — had a terrible fear of being considered nothing. After leading a war against Russia in the 1870s, and being responsible for an Armenian massacre in the 1890s, he became increasingly concerned about how history would portray him. When Abdul found out about the symbol H_2O (which stands for water), he decided to ban all references to the symbol in chemistry books. Why? Because he truly thought H_2O meant 'Hamid is nothing'.

He wasn't the only one who feared the concept of nothing in history. Zero and nothing used to be linked with the concept of void. The Egyptians, the Romans and the Greeks all considered nothing to be synonymous with disorder and chaos. Many civilizations found it hard to accept zero at first. Was it even a number? Zero doesn't multiply like others numbers. For example, one and one equals two. But zero and zero is just zero, so there doesn't seem to be any reason to use the zero in the first place. In addition, zero seems to be a stubborn number that doesn't multiply. This was confusing to people. Moreover, zero doesn't comply with the Axiom of Archimedes, a basic principle of mathematics. The basic rule is that if you add a number to itself, it will exceed itself in magnitude. Hence, zero was a symbol with quite negative associations. This also affected people's fear of emptiness and unexplainable creation myths. Since zero has no substance, it was considered void and therefore equaled chaos.

This fear of nothing is not just something from the past. Nowadays, it's called 'cenophobia'. Not to be confused with the dislike or prejudice against foreigners, xenophobia. Cenophobia is the fear of void, empty spaces or empty rooms. What fascinates me is that a cenophobe believes that there can even be such as a thing as an empty space! An empty space can only be perceived when you're actually there. And when you're there, the room can't be empty! Has anyone ever told these people?

As we humans feel that we're getting smarter every week and technology is taking even greater leaps, I can imagine us becoming increasingly afraid of nothing in a matter of years. In every sense of the word. Afraid of being bored. Afraid to be alone. Similar to years back, when everyone seemed afraid of ghosts. Only now it's just emptiness they fear; the lack of ghosts. Some of us already experience this – I'm sure a deserted self-service gas station isn't a place you'd necessarily prefer to be in the middle of the night. Simply because you know no one is there, but there MIGHT still be something. It's that insecurity that makes it scary. Let's put this into perspective. Would you be afraid in a haunted house, even if a hundred scientists had checked it and confirmed that there is really nothing there? It's often more about a feeling we have and I'm not sure whether a confirmation of nothing being there ever really helps.

Being afraid of nothing is also considered to be a cool thing. It can mean that there's literally nothing that can make you scared. Superheroes seem to use this bold statement a lot. I don't think it's brave at all; to me it's quite scary if nothing makes you scared. It seems to me it's perfectly normal to be scared of some things.

It's what makes us human. If you wouldn't be scared of falling off a cliff, you might not stop just before reaching the edge. People forget that fear is also a useful warning mechanism. I don't have to explain that if you're scared of nothing, you're also a cenophobe right?

"SOME PEOPLE
NEED HELP FINDING
NOTHING."

(8)

WE TEND TO SEARCH FOR NOTHING, A LOT

If I would ask you to do absolutely nothing – for 10 minutes every day – would you say yes? You would probably think it's a waste of time. Well, you might think otherwise after the following. Because, without being aware of it, you already do something similar quite often.

Let's say I want you to find nothing. Do you close your eyes and see the black and the dark? Or would you not be able to find what you're looking for? Let's focus on the latter. Since this is something that happens on a daily basis. Say you're trying to find that one pen you love to write with. You've lost it somewhere in the house. You've searched everywhere and it's simply nowhere to be found. You look under the table, nothing. Under the couch, nothing. In your bag, nothing. Congratulations! You found nothing. It's everywhere.

Overall, we search about ten minutes for an average of nine items each day. In just one year, that's 3,650 hours of searching for nothing! In fifty years, we find more than a hundred thousand nothings. This is something we've already been doing for decades. Ever since we've surrounded ourselves with more stuff that can get lost. I was one of those people who could get really annoyed. I used my Apple Watch to find my iPhone and when I found my iPhone I used it to find my keys, which are attached to a handy GPS keychain. I've always thought, with all the things we've invented, we still haven't found simple ways to find our stuff back easily. I am notorious for my whirlwind approach, just throwing everything on the floor until I find that one lost item. Unless you provide every possession you have with a GPS tag, you'll find yourself searching for things and finding nothing every day. A regular morning for me begins with finding the right shoes, then my bag, some documents I printed and a sticky note that refuses to stick where I've put it. However, I wasn't aware of all the nothings I find in one day.

Sometimes, we find something back again. But replaceable things, like pens, are hard to find back. How do we make these things disappear? No one knows. It's some sort of great magic that comes with humanity. I've realized that all this searching for something and finding nothing is completely useless. All this lost time can be put to much better use.

Searching for something and finding nothing is the most stupid thing ever, because nothing is everywhere. You don't have to search for it. You can close your eyes, cover your ears, stare at the word nothing or use your imagination; it's just there. Many people think it's a ridiculous thing to do. To me it's more ridiculous to search for something you're not going to find anyway. Finding nothing is often considered to be a disappointment – and I completely disagree. It's privilege to find nothing, because only few people are aware of this. You have to be a bit creative and crazy. Nevertheless, it does make you look at things and nothings differently. When you find nothing instead of something, it feels so much more rewarding. Obviously, it's something that is easily overlooked. To give you an example, I found nothing when I searched for a book that would help me understand what nothing is and can be. I first found nothing and, just out of curiosity, I developed an idea out of that. That's also the moment I decided to write it myself.

Some people need a bit of help with finding nothing. I recommend my book *Write Nothing In Here*. It will help you find nothing, every day in a different way. It's a think book to help you create thoughts and things out of nothing. It's particularly effective for people who don't use their creative brain on a daily basis. To give you a glimpse of the book: write down 5 things you know nothing about. Have a look at your notes and let them inspire you to come up with ideas or new angles for solving a problem. It's a really simply and effective method to help you see other things that might be inspiring. Another good exercise is to ignore everything around you. We often forget how much we're influenced by the things we see and experience every day, the world we live in, or the culture we're part of. When you ignore where you are now, what country you are in, or what you've seen today, you're more open to new things.

"WHEN WE DO NOTHING, WE JUST SLOWLY DIE."

9

DOING NOTHING
CAN KILL YOU

We all know that doing something stupid can cost you your life. However, doing nothing is even more dangerous. In fact, it can kill you. Sometimes even faster than doing something can. Let me explain. Imagine you're sitting on a chair. You decide to do nothing for days. You don't eat, you don't move. You simply sit there. Assuming you don't die of boredom, depending on your metabolism and the climate you're in, doing nothing would kill an average person in 8 to 10 days. In colder circumstances you would probably die faster, because your body needs warmth and this costs more energy to generate, which you get from eating.

Crazy fact: people who work in offices tend to sit still for more than 75% of their working day. In a year, that must be more than one thousand hours of sitting still. I'm probably overreacting a little bit, but I bet you're sitting on your cheeks while reading this. Doesn't this concern you? Some scientists claim it's even more dangerous than smoking.

Let's look at people who survived this sitting around and doing nothing. They can survive without food or water for a long period of time. People from India seem to be particularly good at this. Gandhi fasted for twenty-one days in his seventies. Then there's the amazing story of Prahlad Jani, a religious man in India, who claims to have lived without food and water for over seventy years. Two teams of investigators have tried to resolve the mystery and still haven't got a clue. Some say he's tricking us all. Jani, however, is remarkably cooperative with these investigations. Since my roots are half Indian, I thought it was a proprietary element of my genes to fast for long periods of time. So I tried it for myself and it lasted for about 59 minutes.

Back to the boredom thing. Since food isn't all that keeps you going. A research among London civil servants (who seem to be extremely bored at times) showed that bored people are 2.5 times more likely to die of a heart problem. Not sure whether it's true or not (I tend to question research), but we can agree that boredom doesn't really contribute to a healthy lifestyle.

For example, if you're bored, you're likely to watch TV and we all know how healthy TV dinners are. With the increase of TV streaming services like Netflix, I can imagine that people feel more like they're in control and are therefore less bored, but it's actually the same. We should have Netflix or YouTube dinners by now, tailored to the I-decide-whatever-I-want-to-see generation.

It appears that the only way not to die while doing nothing is to infinitely meditate. They once found a mummified monk in lotus position in Mongolia. He was meditating and they claim he never really died. Because he is meditating, he simply remains in a deep state of meditation. There are several cases of people in India who have been found dead whilst meditating, but if you look up this story it's amazing how well-preserved this monk's body looks. Remember this when you're bored. When we humans do nothing, unless we're called Gandhi or Prahlad Jani, we just slowly die.

"IT'S ABOUT
EMBRACING THE
IDEA THAT NOTHING
IS YOURS."

10

WE NEED
NOTHING

The average consumer in the west buys a new car every five years and goes on holiday almost every year. He/she also buys a new phone every one to two years, uses 656 soap bars, and eats 12,129 hamburgers in his/her lifetime. Roughly, he/she consumes 25 tons of food and uses about 15 tons of plastic throughout his/her life. With an average of four hours a day, he/she spends 12 years of his/her life behind the TV.

These numbers are based on nothing, but let's assume they're true. Virtually our whole life is dedicated to buying things, owning things and, when we get older, selling things – so we can buy more. Our possessions can be so overwhelming that there's now a new group of people on the verge of taking over the world: the minimalists.

The minimalists made the shift from being rich with material things to gaining rich experiences by using their principle of living more and wanting less. I'm talking about stories of couples that sell everything they possess and then decide to live a humble life in Asia or somewhere else, enjoying every minute of the day.

In today's world, traveling with nothing has become a trend. It's really hot and hip to travel the world with the least amount of stuff. Some call this minimalist travel. I always imagined those travelers would be naked, sitting with their buttocks on an airplane seat – ready for their minimalist adventure. They search the world for naked beaches and walk around with their crested dogs. Going through customs would be so much easier, and traveling light would finally find its real meaning.

Owning nothing is much more than walking around buck naked. It's about embracing the idea that nothing is yours.

Your house, the pants you're wearing, and maybe even your wife. It's more than a crazy thought, though. If we borrowed more from each other, it would potentially save us a lot more money. And I'm not suggesting we should live like Mormons in a closed community. I'm talking about the idea of everything being a collective possession.

Could we humans be happy if we owned nothing but our bodies? With the latest developments in music and data, we can already see that it's not important to own things anymore. Having access to them is far more important. Wherever you are in the world, your songs and documents need to travel with you. Not on your USB or by synching them on your device, but simply by always having access to them.

This future, I guess, will be a mixture of zero ownership with a pinch of Zen. Possessing things will become completely useless, only done by collectors or museums and really greedy people. Having access to data and adding to an eternal stream of information will change our lives drastically. Moments and memories will automatically be saved, in whatever format we prefer. We will enjoy our past, while experiencing the now.

We actually don't need that much, do we? What things do we own and what do we actually need? Do we really need an iPad? Or a smart watch? I have both and have noticed that, in the beginning, I used them on daily basis. However, after a month or two, I forgot about them. The media themselves became irrelevant; I was only interested in the results they promised. Such as being able to do my work after office hours without getting a headache. Or handy shortcuts on my wrist to save time. This had nothing to do with these devices; they were substitutes for the real solution. Which actually lies in using this concept of nothing more. By taking a step back, having a moment of silence, or staring at a blank canvas. This is what we really need; nothing. Perhaps if we could integrate this practice, then we would work more efficiently and become less frustrated with technology that seeks to fill this gap.

"DOING NOTHING FOR THE ENVIRONMENT IS SOMETHING EVEN THE LAZIEST PERSON WOULD LOVE."

11

DOING NOTHING CAN SAVE THE ENVIRONMENT

Al Gore did a great job. Flying all over the world – using the most pollutional mode of transport – and telling its population we shouldn't be polluting our environment. I love it. Seriously, I do. Not just because I like pointing out a man's contradictions. The fact is, we are all talking about it. It means something. We're more aware of the environment than ever. In addition, we now actually have a wealth of words that express that. Such as footprint, indicating the amount of impact a product has on the environment. Or upcycle, making something better and of a higher quality than its original state. The environment is embedded in our minds. It's almost as though Al invented environmental change. There might be one thing that he has left out of this story. Something Al Gore forgot, but could save us all. It's that one thing that would make the world a better place. It would solve wars and disruptions on Earth, and could make each of us redesign life in a sustainable way.

Do nothing – for the environment.

It's as simple as that. If we go out less, eat less, produce less, drive less, spend less, we would also produce less waste and, with that, less pollution. If you do nothing for an hour every day, you're helping the environment. It's really simple and I just need 5 words to explain it. I don't need an airplane to tell this story to the world either. I can imagine I might not get much support for this, because I'm basically telling everyone to buy less and consume less. This would bring back the demand for products and eventually make factories worldwide distribute less. But they would also cause less pollution. It's a long shot, I know, since it's in our human nature to go to bigger supermarkets and buy 5 shampoos for the price of one. Looking at myself, I really shouldn't leave the water tap open for that long. And I don't need a closet full of doomsday prep goods either. These are all things we can change ourselves.

Doing nothing for the environment is something even the laziest person in the world would love. I think that's really our target group here, lazy human beings who don't give a rat's ass. Now they can contribute to a bigger thing simply by doing nothing (or less). Don't wash your clothes, ever. Just reuse your plate. Turn your underwear inside out. But please, please always wash yourself. Never stop doing that. This increases the chance of getting a job (or keeping your current one). Not washing yourself would be really bad for the economy. Although, perhaps the perfume industry would benefit from this trend?

I guess doing nothing would make us all happier human beings. When your other half arrives home and you've done nothing all day, you can now say that you've contributed to the environment. That you have a bigger goal in life; doing nothing all day. When someone says you're nothing but useless, you can say that you're actually being very useful by contributing to a better environment. When someone says you know nothing, you can say that you know that doing nothing actually helps the environment.

On a bigger scale, if we could introduce a worldwide 'do nothing day' on which people would not be allowed to use their cars, fly, or buy new things in stores, but just eat leftovers or things they already have in their homes, imagine how much energy this would save? Symbolically, this should be the day after New Year's Eve. It's already a boring day to a lot of people. Now, we would simply make good use of this day. I believe there are already several initiatives like this; movements that are sort of against our mass consumption behavior. I think it would only be truly effective if everyone in the world contributed to this day. Which would be the big challenge. Doing nothing isn't something people generally do; this in itself can be an eye-opening experience for a lot of people.

"GETTING HIGH
ON NOTHING IS
ONE OF THE MOST
ADDICTIVE THINGS
IN THE WORLD."

(12)

YOU CAN GET HIGH ON NOTHING

Here's the chapter that many people must have been waiting for; how to get high by doing nothing? It has nothing to do with smoking banana leafs, hula hooping for hours or a breathe-in-breathe-out sex experience. All of these things are really fun, but they still take a lot of effort. I've been looking at things that take virtually no effort, or no effort at all, and can still get you in a trance or higher state. I've mentioned meditation before, but I'm going to leave that out for now, since it's the most obvious way of getting high, but certainly not the easiest. Some wouldn't even call it getting high.

I was intrigued by an experiment that served fake alcohol and got people drunk. Simply giving people tonic and lime is about as far as you need to go. Of course, the researchers in the experiment had claimed that it was a vodka cocktail. What's so striking, is that the participants' IQ performance became lower and their judgment got impaired. This is really interesting. Should someone be allowed to drive when they think they're drunk? What about pregnant women? Could they participate in this experiment or would their baby experience the effect, too? I do know that a night out would be so cheap. It got me wondering whether the same would be possible for drugs. Indeed, I found out that there are different ways to get high without doing anything.

The easiest way is to stop doing something we usually do every day: sleeping. It might sound like a big joke, but researchers from the University of California, Berkeley and Harvard Medical School examined the brain of two groups of people; one that had slept normally and another group that had not slept in thirty hours. Everyone was asked to rate pictures of happy things, such as rabbits and ice cream, as neutral or positive. The ones who skipped a night of sleep rated the images more positively than the other well-rested half of the participants. When they measured their brain activity, the pleasure center (driven by dopamine) of the all-nighters was greatly boosted after missing a night's sleep.

I'm not sure in what way they conducted the research, but one of the researchers mentioned that normal events evoked exaggerated emotional reactions in the sleep-deprived group. For instance, feeling joyfully happy only at the sight of an image of a cookie. This sounds quite similar to what happens under the influence of drugs, when your memory, attention, and problem-solving abilities seem to be affected as well. Therefore, if you want to get high, just skip a night of sleep.

The other option is listening to binaural beats. No, this is not a new Beats By Dre headphone; it is in fact an auditory illusion that one can experience, similar to the feeling of using drugs. Apparently, there's a whole math construction behind this, but it basically comes down to hearing a different frequency in each ear and using tones that are out of the ordinary. I hadn't heard of this before, but there's a whole world of binaural web shops on the Internet that sell these tracks. When I tried one of these tracks called Ecstasy, it actually made me feel really uncomfortable and nervous. As with every drugs, the environment seems to be important. So have a go at it and download your high in two clicks. You'll find out that getting high on nothing is one of the most fascinating things in the world.

The final way to do nothing and get high is to use hypnosis. It's not a scientifically proven method, but extremely interesting. A hypnotist cannot put a new experience of drugs in your mind, but he/she can bring you back to a drugs experience in the past. So, this can only work if you've used drugs before. A hypnotist can get you back to that feeling, memory, and deep experience of being in trance, having a dry mouth, and even feeling dizzy. You'll remember every detail of that vivid experience. While most people think hypnosis is used to turn people into gorilla's or chickens, it's actually a well-known therapeutic method.

"DON'T CALL YOURSELF LUCKY WHEN YOU HAVE GOOD EYESIGHT; YOU'RE STILL UNABLE TO SEE NOTHING."

SOME
PEOPLE CAN SEE
NOTHING

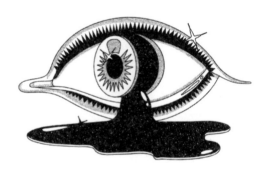

There are thousands of people who can see nothing. Some are born with it and others can't see because of an injury or disease. For people who can see it's hard to imagine what it's like. The ones who were born blind never had visual references for objects and people. And the ones who turned blind have references for things they've seen in the past. When you think at what you've seen in the past and how things changed throughout time, you know this memory might not always be accurate – but it's the only thing they can hold on to. Just like dolphins do, the blind sometimes use sound and touch to form an image of an object. As sound is reflected of these objects, they can identify what those are.

Don't call yourself lucky just yet, because when you have good eyesight, you're still unable to actually see nothing. We haven't developed our other senses as much as a people who were born blind and therefore don't have as much imagination. We don't have the same rich sensory experience each time we close our eyes; for us it's just closing our eyes.

The closest thing for us with eyesight would be whatever the closest thing to nothing is. And that's the tiniest thing we can perceive. So what's the tiniest thing we can see? What appears to be a scientific question is really just a matter of figuring out how far along we are with microscopes. It would be totally illogical for me to answer this question, since I'm not a scientist. Then again, it would be completely illogical to write a book about nothing, right?

This is the kind of question we can all answer if we do a little bit of research. We simply have to look for the smallest visible particle of matter the world has ever found. Ooooh, if that's all! Let's start big and then zoom in. The biggest thing in the world isn't a giant man-made Piñata. It's also not a building in Dubai, and it isn't the world's biggest living thing, fungus, which I've come to understand can stretch as far as 3.5 miles. It's the world itself - come on, you could have come up with that! Now zoom in a bit further and you see that sand is considered to be an important building block on Earth.

As a kid, I thought that sand was the smallest thing in the world. Until I learned that is actually consists of particles, which unlocks the world of atoms. I then found out about protons (positively charged particles), neutrons (with a neutral charge or no charge), and electrons (with a negative charge). Each particle is like a little battery, held together with different kinds of energy. I'm not any more of an expert on this than you are, but these proton thingies are made of 3 quarks each. So far, these quark friends seem to be indivisible. Perhaps, by the time you read this book, they have already found a way to divide them into even smaller particles. For now, this seems to be a stopping point. Isn't there anything in the world smaller than these quarks scientists talk about? The answer appears to be no. The closest thing to nothing is something indivisible. And that, my friend, is something we can't even see. So how do we know it's there? We know because they make up the particles of things we can see.

It doesn't stop there. We now know that even when a box is empty, with all the energy inside we can't say there's nothing in it. The closest thing to nothing that my crazy brain can imagine cannot be found in science. Rather, it consists of a way of looking at things and no-things. If you look at everything around you, you can consider each individual item to be nothing. I'm sure this isn't really the exciting answer you were hoping for, so I've been digging a bit deeper. For people who can see, the closest thing to seeing nothing is a feeling. Something that is so present, but still too elusive. You can't see it, but you can describe it. When you're in a packed train, no one would notice it's there, except you.

There's also another approach to seeing nothing. It's the story of the Native Americans that weren't able to see the boats of Columbus in the sea, even though they were in plain sight. The ships were said to be outside the Natives' mental framework, leading to them simply not being able to perceive them. If you see something that you have no conceptual framework for, you don't actually register it. The same goes for nothing; there's no framework in our minds yet to see nothing. We can only think of something that is not there.

"WHEN SOMEONE TELLS YOU THERE'S NOTHING WRONG WITH YOU, DON'T TAKE IT AS A COMPLIMENT."

(14)

NOTHING IS WRONG WITH YOU

We are funny human beings. If a person tells you the grass is blue, you dispute it. If a group tells you, you reconsider it. If the whole world claims it, you start to believe it. We're fascinated by other species – but the way we humans lie to ourselves is way beyond bananas.

There's this experiment in which a group of people were shown a card with a line on it. This is then followed by a card with three lines on it. They were asked to say aloud which of the three lines matched the line on the first card in length. Easy-peasy. However, prior to the experiment, all participants got instructions to respond in the same incorrect way, except for one person. This was the actual guinea pig. This person didn't get any instructions whatsoever. He first gave his own honest opinion. Our lab rat started by disagreeing and stating his opinion out loud. Whilst the others followed instructions and all gave the wrong answer, our test subject started to give incorrect answers too. This is truly spectacular! These types of experiments show that people step away from the truth when the majority of their peers have a different opinion. Perhaps we need to look at elections differently? To me it shows that if the majority is convinced of something, it's not hard to influence the rest. If I can make the world believe that nothing is something, then the sky is the limit.

There are also ways to heal people with nothing. It's been proven that a placebo can be highly effective. You know, those fake medicines that have positive effects, because people think they are real. In one study, the effect of a placebo medicine for asthma patients was investigated. When they asked the patients how they felt after using the placebo inhaler, they told the researchers it had been effective and that they felt relieved. This has everything to do with your expectations. If you think that the person who gives you the medicine is trustworthy and that the medicine will help you it can deliver the same results as a real medicine. I see an opportunity for a new kind of pharmacy with all these placebo medicines. You can pick up your placebo; perhaps we can email it to you?

In addition to this nothing medicine, there's also the Nocebo effect, which is a bit more unpleasant. This means that when you think you're incurably ill, your brain will respond accordingly. It's based on the idea that when you expect something to be bad or have a negative effect, it often will. In one example, someone attempted suicide with 26 pills. These were harmless sugar pills, but the patient believed they were real, as a result of which he experienced low blood pressure and even required injections of fluid to keep him stabilized. It got horribly out of hand.

The truth is, we don't want to be different at all. We want to be normal. That's why we often reassure each other that 'there's nothing wrong with you', because that makes you a normal person. And, boy, don't we just love normal. However, when someone tells you there's nothing wrong with you, don't take this as a compliment. That person is basically saying that it's not OK to be different.

"BECOMING FRIENDS WITH NOTHING ISN'T A SAD THING."

THERE'S A GREAT CHANCE YOU WERE FRIENDS WITH NOTHING

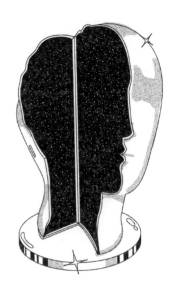

Kids have a great sense of imagination. Unfortunately, this is also the reason parents or teachers don't always take them serious: "Oh, it's nothing, let's not worry 'bout it." And when something is deemed to be nothing, we are not supposed to pay attention to it, are we?

It turns out that half of children between ages 4-12 have, or have had, an imaginary friend. You could argue that the friend is invisible and therefore not real. But let's say we follow Parmenides' principle: that even when something is merely a manifestation of the mind, it's still existent. An imaginary friend can have greater impact than a real friend. Nowadays, our society likes to associate these kinds of phenomena with psychological and social disorders. However, it seems like this not a disorder, but rather an advantage.

Studies show that kids with imaginary companions develop language skills and retain knowledge faster than children without them. Thanks to the conversations with their imaginary friend, these kids practice their linguistic skills more extensively. And all of this, because they're talking to nothing. Imaginary friends also help kids make sense of the world of adults.

What if an imaginary friend could allow adults to make better sense of their world? I mean, I talk to myself all the time. It's a great resource to pitch ideas to, to call on when making big decisions, or to help put a thought into words. When I pitched the idea for this book to my imaginary friend, he instantly loved it. It was hard for me to bring all the cons into perspective, since he's not very critical. After we had a long talk, we finally agreed that a book about nothing isn't something you often come across.

Becoming friends with nothing isn't a sad thing. You're never alone, you can have great conversations about all the things you would like to talk about, share mutual interests, evaluate things, have brainstorms – only a game of tennis would be challenging. One of the benefits of an imaginary friend is that you can give yourself therapy and it's available 24 hours a day! For instance, when you're dealing with things or want to overcome feelings that overwhelm you. You can keep a journal, have an inner dialogue, or just ask your imaginary friend what he would do. It's really cost-effective.

Does this phenomenon belong in a mental institution? Control is the word here. There are guidelines for this, which you shouldn't ignore. Never ever do this with other people around. They will think you're crazy. The quickest way to get out of a situation like this is pretending you're singing a song. Nothing else matters saved me about a hundred times in these kinds of situations. It's easy to become friends with nothing. When we were babies, we did it all the time. We laughed our asses off by ourselves and we didn't need anyone for that. It seems to make a lot of babies happy, so why wouldn't it work for you?

"MOST PEOPLE FIND THE CONCEPT OF INFINITY MORE ACCEPTABLE THAN THAT OF NOTHING."

THERE'S A UNIVERSAL SYMBOL FOR NOTHING

What started as a dot, turned into a separator and years and years later ended up a oval circle. All of this didn't happen overnight. Was it the Mayans who invented the zero? The Greeks? The Egyptians? The Babylonians? Perhaps the Hindus? Or did it come from the Sumerian culture? Each in their own way, the various cultures contributed to this symbol of nothingness. Some say it's a symbol that was heavily influenced by one culture and then passed on to another. Others say the Mayans and Hindus invented it independently. It's way too long ago for us to be bothered with the details.

However, the oldest known mention of the numeral zero can be found in the Jain cosmological text from India entitled the Lokavibhâga, dated 458 AD. Indians love to focus on the emptiness of things and have found a way to get to nothing by meditating. The Hindu god Shiva, who is a destroyer and creator, even represents nothingness. To me, this demonstrates that there's a certain openness towards the concept of nothing in these cultures. It follows that it then made perfect sense to create a symbol for it.

Of course, the zero symbol itself isn't all that interesting, it's how you use it. I've been told that Indian mathematician and astronomer Brahmagupta was the first to come up with a rule system for computing with zero. Then the Persian mathematician, al-Khwarizmi, introduced the numeral in the 8th century, and the Arabs brought zero to Europe. The Greeks and Romans weren't fond of this symbol, to say the least. Why would someone change their ancestors' numeral system? They went a step further and even introduced a law that forbade bankers from using zero, or any of the new Arab numerals in their accounts. Maybe they should have talked to sultan Abdul Hamid II about it.

When I visited Chichén Itza, a pyramid and world wonder based in Yucatan, Mexico, it was inspiring to see that the contemporaries of the pyramid had developed and used a numeral system in their own way. For the Mayans, the balance between sunrise and sunset seemed to be centered at Chichén Itza, which is why they considered this to be the center of the universe. The Mayans were observers of space and life. At first, their calendar made more sense than any western calendar. After all, that one was created at a time when the zero didn't even exist. Nowadays, we also question their calendar, but I'm not so sure whether we westerns – who in those days didn't even have a zero in our calendars – should really have a say in this.

I bet you can't find the infinity symbol on your keyboard. The irony is that most people can find the concept of infinity more acceptable than that of nothing. The idea of zero – which I'm certain is a much more commonly used symbol – is nevertheless harder to accept and understand for most people. To me, the infinity symbol (∞) seems nothing more than two zeros attached to each other. No one seems to have written anything about this, nor is the connection between the two commonly referred to. Someone once told me that a googol, a 1 with a hundred zeros behind it, is what the well-known search engine got its name from, based on the idea of infinite information. Still, even this isn't infinite. I do believe that the zero and the infinity symbol have something to do with each other. They are just not the exact opposites of each other. Infinity doesn't grow, and neither does zero. Infinity is also not a real number, but more of a concept. And finally, it plays with the idea of having no end. And doesn't the symbol for zero seem to have no end either? Isn't that a more succinct representation of infinity? It might stand for a void of something, but is there always such a thing as one void or are there multiple? Moreover, if zero is the end or beginning, then where does infinity start? I believe in the infinity of zero.

Whatever you think of these symbols, I think it's funny that we first created a symbol that represents something we didn't really believe in. Something we feared, even. In other cultures, zero stood for the ultimate state of being. Throughout the years, zero has developed into something with a negative association again. It doesn't interfere with our beliefs as much as it did in ancient times, but now it's more about not having anything or the absence of things. For example, when you have zero on your bank account, you are considered to be poor. I think we should reconsider this attitude.

Let's say we want to add more value to a zero. What would the effect be of a zero Euro coin? Perhaps we could combine it with 2 Euro coins, so that they would jointly make 20. It could become a new counting system in which zero coins would basically adds value to any random Euro or dollar coin. You would only need one dollar and six zero coins to become a millionaire. In this example, the zero coin becomes the most valuable one. Admittedly, the economy would probably collapse, bankers would get some major headaches, and we would spend way too much money at once. Look on the bright side. The economy has already collapsed, bankers already have major headaches, and we already spend way too much at once. So there isn't really any reason not to do it.

"WE AUTOMATICALLY ASSUME THAT THE SOUND OF NOTHING IS SILENCE."

YOU CAN'T
HANDLE THE SOUND
OF NOTHING

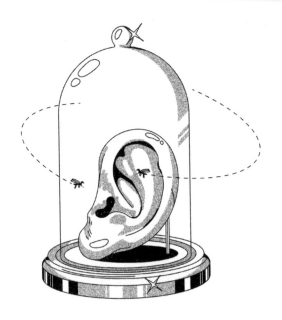

In space, there's no sound. At least, we can't perceive it with the ears we have. That's what scientists say, because apparently sound can't move through a vacuum. I have never been in space, so they can basically sell me any story they want. Imagine a massive explosion in the middle of space. You wouldn't be able to hear a thing. Without getting into the whole scientific side of things, the same principle applies to people who are deaf. They are surrounded by sound, but they can't hear it. I wondered whether they might have a sound memory. Might they be able to have a tune or rhythm stuck in their head, without ever having heard a sound? What would it sound like if a hearing-impaired person created a song? These are things I can't stop wondering. So I asked someone who is unable to hear about what sound means to her.

The person I interviewed has been deaf since she was 1 year old. This makes a sound memory almost impossible. What fascinated me was how she described the sound of silence. "My eyes function like ears. I see how people respond, become angry, move, and get happy. The waves in the sea, a tree in the wind, cars passing by – I hear nothing and still my imagination gently flows with the things around me. I know that people who hear sounds are also commonly distracted by them. I only hear through whatever I feel in silence. Whether I would love to hear one day? I think I'd go nuts. I prefer the feeling of sound; that seems nicer to me".

Wow, the feeling of sound? I don't even know what that is. It reminds me of when I listen to music. Getting chills up my spine and really getting emotional sometimes. But that's not what she meant. She actually talked about the feeling of it that she experiences with every (other) sense in her body. Sometimes it's the vibrations in combination with her imagination. And other times it's a visual indication that she gets. For example, when something falls on the floor, she imagines what it sounds like. Visual indications give her a reason to attach sound to what she sees. For instance, a glass falling or a door being slammed. Feeling sound is something completely different than hearing it.

One study found that deaf people are able to sense vibrations in the same part of the brain that others use for hearing. That's kind of surprising to me, since it sounds like a completely different experience. It might be the same part in the brain that we use, but I think the feeling of sound is something us people with functional hearing will never fully understand. Music artist Pharrell Williams mentioned in an interview that he experiences a phenomenon that he calls seeing sounds. It's not just the title of one of his albums, but it's actually a way in which he experiences music. When he hears music, he basically sees it in color. For him it's the only way he can identify what something sounds like. It's really interesting that there's a name for this, too. It's called synesthesia, a neurological phenomenon in which the stimulation of certain senses automatically triggers the stimulation of other senses, too. It sounds like something you could easily get distracted by, but apparently it's pretty normal for the people that have it.

We automatically assume that the sound of nothing is silence. Beethoven became deaf, too, and still created numerous pieces of music. Even his disability did not prevent him from composing music. He obviously had a huge imagination to be able to create sound pieces.

Silence merely proves that we humans are not equipped with full hearing ability. Can you honestly say that when you're in a silent room, with all the doors closed, the tiny bugs in the carpet are not making a sound? Of course they are. We just can't hear them. Perhaps the closest thing to hearing nothing would be the sound of everything. Like a light spectrum that produces white light, but is actually a combination of every colored light source there is. When it comes down to sound, we certainly wouldn't be able to hear anything anymore the moment we hear everything.

Orfield Labs is a company that conducts research into acoustics and vibration. They've created what they refer to as the quietest place on earth. While an average 'quiet room' has 30 decibels of sound, this space holds the Guinness World Record of -9 decibels. How does this work? They created an anechoic chamber, which looks like a massive sound studio with lots of wood texture to create a noise cancellation system. It's been said to be so quiet, you can hear your own organs. Blood pumping through your heart, your stomach digesting your food, swallowing. Everything you would normally not hear in that space is amplified. It's used for testing products like LED lights and it's been said to be a horrible experience. Of course, we're surrounded by sound all the time and we're not even aware of it. Most of the time we ignore it. It might be fun for a minute, but the quietest room in the world is apparently a really scary experience. After a while, you start to hallucinate and hear sounds that aren't even there. I guess this is what nothing sounds like.

"NOTHING IS
THE MOST
VALUABLE THING
ONE CAN BUY."

(18)

SELLING NOTHING SELLS MORE

An average person is confronted with about three thousand advertising messages a day. If we don't count inhabitants of the jungle, that is. Sometimes the messages are rational: buy, donate, submit, share, or download. Sometimes emotional: enjoy more, smell good, eat healthy, or whatever other hook those crazy folks can think up. I'm one of those crazy folks by the way. I've been working in advertising for almost a decade, which doesn't say much, except for the fact that in advertising time I'm like 67 years old. I always wondered what it would be like if we advertised nothing.

I don't mean empty billboards, but selling the idea of nothing.

Would it make you feel better if ads didn't sell things but no-things? It would make people suspicious; I'm sure I would be. "Why on Earth are they wishing me a good day? What are they saying, that they're not explicitly saying?" Imagine a Nike ad that says: "Just don't do it". Would that encourage society to become lazy and unambitious? Would this promote a negative habit? Or would this actually be appreciated?

In the example of 'just don't do it', you might consider this a propaganda message from a controlling society. Who decides what you can and cannot do? However, doesn't that go for 'just do it' as well? I mean, I decide whether I want to do something or not. If Nike would advertise 'just do nothing', could we rationalize that into a lifestyle? I'm sure we could. It could be a message about freedom and taking a step back from our busy lives. We could also send out a message to turn nothing into something; to do something out of nowhere.

What if they didn't sell anything? Not a product, not a statement, no logo. The ads would just say something like: "Nothing". People would create their own theories and thinking behind it. That it might be some attempt to engage with the audience on a deeper level. While in fact, the message might just have been there – not to bother you, not to inspire you, and not even to hold your interest. It's just there, for no reason. I guess that's the fine line between applied creativity and art. Art evokes multiple emotions, whereas an ad eventually leads to a purchase. The messages should be somewhere in the middle.

I would like to challenge brands to advertise nothing. To not make people buy, see, or do stuff – but just make them do nothing. Wouldn't it be great if a company would advertise to do nothing today, just because it makes us feel good? Without this being part of a campaign, bigger concept, or marketing idea; just because it would be a nice experiment and it would be really entertaining to see this come alive.

Next to advertising the idea of doing nothing, I'm extremely curious whether I could find a buyer for nothing. It's like the ultimate nothing experiment. I want to put the biggest nothing up for auction. The product would be nothing you can see and nothing you can touch. It would be nothing you can download either. It would have no physical form and it would also not be special service you get. The nothing that I'm thinking about selling is simply nothing. After all, buying nothing is the most valuable purchase one can make. Nevertheless, it's the biggest nothing.

Nothing is the most valuable thing one can buy. While most people think that nothing is just nothing, this nothing is huge. I'm not even sure if you could carry this nothing home, let alone hold it in your hands. On the other hand, it's everything everyone hasn't got. It's something unique and it's basically like owning the world, only then in the form of nothing. On my website booksaboutnothing.com I would like to auction this nothing and sell it to the highest bidder. You can leave your details behind and put up an offer. I will notify the winner and will publicly announce it. There will be an official moment where I symbolically hand out the nothing to the buyer. I would love to hear what inspired the buyer to buy nothing and what he or she will do with it. You would also be able to make a donation to nothing. This can be a small amount of 1 euro or 1 dollar. Curious what I will do with the earnings? I will donate the money to nothing of course. I will invest it in an exposition about nothing, something I'm sure everyone would love to see.

"DOING THINGS
OUT OF NOWHERE
ISN'T REALLY
SOMETHING OUR
SOCIETY LIKES."

19

THINGS CAN HAPPEN OUT OF NOWHERE

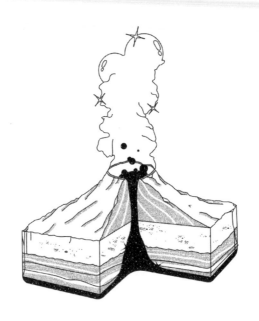

Last year, my mind wandered off while I stood on an escalator at the airport. While I was contemplating what to have for dinner, a sturdy woman fell down and, like a rolled roast, got wrapped up in her bags. She took me, and the people behind me, down with her. Luckily for us, five people down the line she was caught, which stopped her fall. It looked like a funniest home video, but eventually we all got back up and I asked her what had happened. "I don't know, I fell out of nowhere!" To which I answered: "Really? I think you tripped over your bag." Of course, she knew this too, but in that moment she wasn't able to process what had just happened. So, therefore, she shamelessly used the word nowhere – as if she had fallen due to nothing.

Can things happen out of nowhere – and thus out of nothing? Stephen Hawking thinks the Big Bang occurred out of nowhere, because there was no time prior to this event. Well, if this is true, that's great news. I reckon this means that more great things could happen out of nowhere. For instance, I could suddenly start dancing on the table in the middle of writing this. I guess it all has to do with how we define something happening out of nowhere.

Our world doesn't really condition us to do things out of nowhere. We try to make people plan as much as we can, so we can prepare. It's apparent in the simplest things, such as meal planning. In the mornings, afternoons, and evenings. It seems so logical to do that. If you work, you have at least two meals at home; breakfast and dinner. People usually only have lunch during office hours. This saves time and money for companies. But who says this is good for your health? Maybe it's better to eat 5 times a day, small bites. On a bigger scale, we also plan our lives and what we spend. Due to things like being able to buy a house when you have enough career security, marriage, or a pension. Many things are decided for us.

I'm not judging this, by the way. It's fine, and a lot of people need those clear paths in life. It's also very convenient. Imagine one million people waking up tomorrow and thinking: "I'm going to do whatever I want to do. Without any preparation whatsoever, I'm going to quit my job and just do the first thing that comes to mind." Our day-to-day system is not built for worldwide impulsiveness. Getting stuck in traffic is just a reminder how stuck we are in the system. Doing things out of nowhere isn't really something our society likes. There are rules for doing things spontaneously.

Some events we can't make rules for. With over five hundred volcanoes worldwide, every year at least fifty of them erupt. It's one of the biggest natural events that can happen out of nowhere. Some of them are silent for decades and others erupt without any warning. You would think that we would have figured this out by now, but it isn't as easy as you might think. Seismometers might track the increase of magma and we might be able to keep on eye on different levels of gas, but each volcano is unique. The best way is to constantly monitor a volcano, even if it might take hundreds of years for one to erupt. We are able to predict an eruption when it's just days ahead, but not months.

The same goes for lightning strikes. There's a one to ten thousand chance that lightning will strike you. It seems so unlikely and something we still can't get our heads around. We are able to predict when lightning will strike and sometimes in what area. We're still not able to predict where exactly. This is slightly worrying, since they predict that climate change will increase lightening strikes with 50% by 2100. There's one person who might be able to tell us something about these events that happen out of nowhere. There's no need to worry, unless your name is Roy Sullivan. He was a United States park ranger and is said to have experienced seven lightning strikes, surviving all of them. It might just be a made-up story, but there's one photo on the web where you see Roy holding his burned hat. Unfortunately, Roy died at the age of 71 from a self-inflicted gunshot wound.

"THE ONLY PERSON WHO UNDERSTANDS WHAT IT FEELS LIKE TO FEEL NOTHING IS PROBABLY A PSYCHOPATH."

20

IT'S POSSIBLE TO FEEL NOTHING

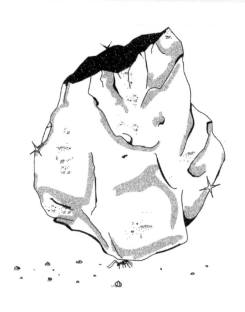

Congenital insensitivity to pain has nothing to do with your genitals, but it's a rare condition that one out of a million people have. These are people that can't feel pain. Mosquito bites, lifting a hot glowing pan with your bare hands, or even a kick in the ass by a donkey would go noticed. Apparently, it's a mutation in the gene PRDM12, which causes this condition. In other words, there are no electric signals to the nerves. Obviously, this is something inherited from the parents. I'm extremely curious how they usually find out. Do they drop their kid and then notice she doesn't cry? Or is it when she drinks the hot milk without squinting?

It's one of the most mysterious conditions people can have and, to be honest, I'm not sure it's a condition; perhaps it's an ability. I might be a bit jealous. They are the modern-day X-Men! Imagine an army of these people. Yes, they are mortals, but they would definitely go the extra mile in the field. Not to mention, the handy practicalities that come with it are infinite. Grabbing a hot chicken out of the oven, getting a head butt, hugging a hedgehog – just a few examples of the extraordinary life you could have. The most painful things in life – which I've come to understand are a penile fracture and a bulldozer on your foot – these people wouldn't twitch their eye.

It's not all just fun though. It can be extremely dangerous, especially for kids. You might not feel the fire on your arm, but that doesn't mean you're not burning. You might end up walking around with a broken arm without knowing it. These people are missing warning signs when they're in potentially dangerous situations. Not to mention the dangerous habits you might have, which are hard to unlearn.

Physical pain is just one aspect of being able to feel nothing. Emotions are another. The average person experiences numerous emotions during the day. Missing a deadline, or worse, getting fired – different activities and occasions evoke various emotions. Scientists believe that one out of a hundred people feel nothing. They don't experience emotions. They are called psychopaths. Don't think these are all killers. I'm talking about people who, from a young age, are able to manipulate people and commit acts of relentless cruelty. That doesn't mean they've committed crimes. Simply put, they are mentally not capable of feeling emotion. You probably wouldn't even notice, because they've often learnt how to copy emotional behavior throughout the years. However, they can't actually experience it. It's a fascinating thing, and hard to grasp for anyone who is not a psychopath. The only person who understands what it feels like to feel nothing would probably be a psychopath. These people don't feel fear or distress and therefore can't recognize it in others.

They don't feel remorse either. Which makes it impossible for them to reflect on situations and evaluate their behavior. Several studies show that they do have the ability to feel empathy, but it's just not their normal state of being. As kids we learn to feel sorry when we're hurting someone. These kids can't feel remorse or guilt.

For people like you and me, feeling nothing is impossible. However, you can choose to keep certain feelings at a distance, and limit the extent to which you are affected

"REVERSE
EVOLUTION WILL
KEEP MOVING
FORWARD UNTIL
THERE'S NOTHING
LEFT OF US."

21

NOTHING COMES TO AN END

Apparently, there are people who don't want to accept that nothing is actually something. They think nothing is an end, not a beginning. I bet they skipped the rest of the book just to read this chapter and say 'I told you so'. If you're one of those people, this chapter is for you. I might have neglected you throughout the book, but that's just because I've been so busy with nothing.

Obviously, you're a believer of nothing and think that nothing is just an empty word. You're convinced that nothing is just nothing. You might have substation for and proof that nothing is nothing, and nothing more. Fine. You know what, let's go with that thought for a minute. Let me convince you for the last time. If nothing is really what you think it is, then there's NOTHING that can convince you to think differently about it.

Am I right? Nothing in the world can change your crazy mind about nothing. There's nothing that can influence your opinion on nothing. In this case, isn't nothing actually something? It stands for everything and everyone but you. It stands for that thing that can't convince you. You see, there's not that much difference between you and me. In the end, nothing unites us. I finally made you realize that nothing is something.

Now that we've made that clear, let's talk about the future of nothing. If nothing is the beginning of things and not a lousy ending, would it have the same meaning in a hundred years from now? Every day we learn more and more about things and technology continues to advance. As we learn more about the somethings in life, we learn about nothings too. The concept of nothing seems more unlikely each minute we think about it. Our best understanding of nothing might not even be the same in a hundred years.

A hundred years from now, nothing will be the ultimate state of being. Once we've invented all the gadgets, experiments, and technological solutions that are out there, we then come to the realization that only thoughts, and not things, make us happy. So then we start to invest in these. These are intangible things. Most of the time you can't see, touch, or hold them.

For example, then you can buy happy thoughts. It can also be a memory, a theory, and even better, a feeling. You would be able to download a specific type of nothing. Like the feeling of buying something new, without actually buying something new. Or the memory of putting your toes in the sand on a sunny beach, without actually going here. Or a theory on how to solve problems without reading books. Life would be so much more tailored to your needs.

As soon as we're able to download things to our brain, we'll unplug ourselves in the weekends. The most precious state of being will not be happiness, but becoming nothing, like an empty USB stick. When a baby is born, we will admire them for their nothing state. We will then simply decide what info it will have and what not. Of course, there's also an evil side to this. After all, you can put the wrong thoughts into someone's head. We'll just forget that for now.

When nothing becomes the new currency, many other things will become redundant. Most people think evolution is something that starts and stops. I like to think it also moves in reverse. Unlike the Neanderthal, we don't have to hunt for dinner or climb trees to survive. If you're a believer of evolution, you must agree that our long arms have become completely useless. You'll notice this most when you lie on your side in bed or when you're sitting in front of your computer and trying to find the right posture behind your desk. Haven't you noticed the self-driving cars, voice control technology, and virtual reality devices? Technology makes it real clear that our arms are not as useful as they were before. We'll slowly go back to where we came from. So how should we show affection without arms? We'll just touch each other's nose. Keep in mind, next time you see someone with a big nose and short arms, you can tell this person's from the future. Thanks to these innovations, our entire bodies will become useless. To start, our arms will become shorter until we look like little t-rexes. Eventually, the rest of our body will shrink down to a tiny single cell. And then (you've probably guessed it already) we'll turn into nothings. Reverse evolution will keep moving forward until there's nothing left of us.

Putting all jokes aside. Nothing never ends; I guess that's what I wanted to steer your mind towards. If you write a book about nothing and fill more than a hundred pages on this subject, it obviously is something. I wanted to show you that there isn't such a thing as nothing. At least not for now. We can argue about this for hours. I guess if you came this far in reading the book, nothing does feed your curiosity. Recognizing nothing represents more than a funny rant to me. It stands for how we choose to see things and no-things. It represents the way we think and put things in boxes. If I can make one person in the world think more about nothing, I've accomplished my goal. Now, go ahead and explore nothing; have a good laugh with it. Tell your friends about it. But above all, don't forget that nothing is whatever you make of it. Thanks, for nothing.

"NOTHING IN THE WORLD IS MORE INTERESTING TO TALK ABOUT THAN NOTHING."

Thanks for nothing.

Thank you Daniël, for designing nothing. Thank you Sarina, for making sense out of nothing. Thank you Mariano, for your energetic nothing. Thank you Mauro, for being part of the early stages of nothing. Thank you John, for inspiring me with nothing. Thank you BIS Publishers, for believing in nothing. Thank you D, for having patience with nothing.

Thank you mom, for inspiring me to be nothing but myself.

Author & concept: Seema Sharma

illustrations by: Mariano Pascual

Design by: Daniël Stadhouder

Publisher:

BISPUBLISHERS

Building Het Sieraad

Postjesweg 1

1057 DT Amsterdam

The Netherlands

T +31 (0)20 515 02 30

bis@bispublishers.com

www.bispublishers.com

ISBN 978 90 6369 441 8

www.booksaboutnothing.com